What is History?

History is the story of people on planet Earth. It begins with human evolution, dating back to 150,000 years and includes everything from politics, faith to cultures. History is a subject that can educate young minds about the past. It can help them decipher the rich past as well as dwell on tragedies.

The importance of history

History is important because it allows us to understand our past, which in turn allows to understand our present. This helps us ascertain why things are the way they are. We need to learn history because it tells us where we came from.

Studying history

History can be read from books; museums can also tell us a lot about our past. Historians study history and write history books. They learn about the past events that have helped shape the present, modern world. They also have fine research skills. They study themes and try to make a complete picture out of it. This enables us to understand our past in a much better manner. Historians aim to provide perspectives, views and analyses to their readers.

Why is history studied?

It is studied because it helps us comprehend the evolution of our world. It enables us to further develop our queries. It also helps shape our opinions. It dives into our roots and gives us information about our ancestors, going all the way back to a simpler time when humans lived in caves. History helps us understand and predict human behaviour.

Father of History

In the fifth century BC, a Greek historian, Herodotus, attempted to put down the events of the past to help people recall and remember the past, and hence is known as the "Father of History".

The First Humans

Although very little is known about early human beings, there has been enough study on the subject to help us generate a few theories and ideas about them. Almost six million years ago, the first humans appeared in East Africa. Back then, they didn't walk on two feet. They walked on all four limbs and often swung from tree to tree. They began to hunt and run away from danger when they finally learnt to walk on two feet. Their bodies changed because they now walked and did not swing from trees. They had relatively smaller brains and were very hairy.

Australopithecus

Fossil skull of Homo Erectus.

Life of the first humans

Early humans were only around three to five feet tall. They lived in caves; there is evidence to prove that caves were their first homes. They ate nuts, roots, yams, insects, fish and meat. It took a few million years for them to evolve into modern humans. They developed bigger brains, and used their tongues and voice to talk. They even lost a lot of their body hair. Over time, they understood how to make fire. Soon, they learnt that fire could keep them warm and help them cook food, making it easier to eat. In time, they learnt how to develop and make their own tools. Their tools were very basic, but more often than not, they used sticks and bones to dig and also defend themselves.

Early humans and their survival techniques

Early humans mainly survived by hunting other animals for food. In order to hunt, they built and used different types of tools made of stones. The flint tools, as they were known, were quite useful to cut and scrape flesh from the hides of animals. Later, humans began making hand axes, which were used to chop wood so that they could light a fire in order to stay warm. The first tools were rough and barely useful, but were improved over the years.

Ancient stone tools.

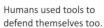

Humans used tools to defend themselves too.

Primitive humans lived outdoors and hunted food.

FAST FACT

There is quite a bit of disagreement about when the first humans migrated to other parts of the globe. There is evidence to prove that some of the first humans moved from Africa almost 1.6 million years ago. Interestingly, it is known that early humans reached Asia only around 460,000 years ago and managed to get to Europe only 400,000 years ago.

Prehistoric Period

201 million years ago

Prehistory describes the time that existed before any recorded history, much before writing was discovered. This was prior to the discovery of the pen or quill!

Long before this period, millions of years ago, dinosaurs roamed on Earth. They were a group of animals that came into being around 201 million years ago during the Jurassic Period.

This period is also known as the "age of reptiles". The word dinosaur means "terrible lizard" and was coined by palaeontologist Richard Owen.

Interestingly, the largest dinosaurs were herbivores or plant-eaters, such as the Brachiosaurus! Other dinosaurs like the Allosaurus or Spinosaurus were carnivores or meat-eaters.

People of the Prehistoric Age

All living beings on this planet belong to and have evolved from the Homo sapiens. These are the people that walked upright and straight. They were called hominids. "Homo sapiens" is the Latin term for "wise human", owing to human beings' developed brains, bipedal gait (where one moves using the two rear limbs or legs) and opposable thumbs. Evidence of this species was found in Africa, Middle East and in Europe.

A Homo sapien man.

Homo sapiens

The Neanderthals, a subspecies of the Homo sapiens, lived between 300,000 to 1,000,000 years ago. They knew how to hunt and build shelters. They were food gatherers and hunters. They also wore animal skins. They used rock and bone to scrape off flesh and fat from skins to use them as clothing. There were certain physical differences such as a larger brain, receding chin and a projecting nose. Most importantly, they stood fully upright.

Climate change

The world climate was witnessing remarkable changes around 1.5 million years ago. The climate became very cold. The drop in temperature led to the four periods of cold temperatures called the Ice Age. Each age is known to have lasted anywhere between 40,000 years and 60,000 years. This impacted man's activities.

People of the prehistoric age

Towards the end of the second "Ice Age", with the climate getting warmer, many tribes of hunters and gatherers travelled to different parts of the continent. These people had no definitive literature, but they believed in some rituals that emphasised the manner in which the dead were buried. Hence, burial chambers with artefacts in them have been found in numerous places including Great Britain.

A stonehenge in Great Britian.

FAST FACT

The first detailed genetic analysis of the Neanderthal genome reveals that some modern humans may have mated with Neanderthals because of which an imprint of the Neanderthal genome was found among modern humans. In fact, biologists say that about 1–4 per cent of the present day human genome was derived from the Neanderthals!

Art of the Prehistoric Age

The prehistoric art is the oldest form of art, appearing much before literature or sculpting.

Around 20,000 BCE, human beings had settled in all the different parts of the globe and various art forms were discovered from all the different continents from Africa to Europe. From cave paintings in Lascaux and Chauvet in France to the engravings of humans in Asia to the rock art in Australia, the art during this age gives us a glimpse of the life of that period.

Cave painting

The Lascaux cave paintings were made with brushes that were made from the fur of animals. Artists from the Palaeolithic age used five different colours including black, violet, yellow, red and brown. Most art that can be recognised dates back to 15,000 BCE and it generally depicted animals, humans and certain symbols. With people engaging in farming activities, art of domestic animals, maps and other landscapes made their presence felt. Pots with different decorations were also made. However, despite this, ceramics were only utilised for domestic purposes since the sixth millennium.

Terracotta vases and goblet bowls are examples of this art.

Children also painted

There has been some evidence of children also using the medium of art to express themselves some 13,000 years ago. In France, the Rouffignac caves have markings called "finger flutings" made by a child, where the art consists of simple lines. The lines have some symbolic meaning. These flutings or meandering lines depict the everyday lives of the people of this time. Some are shaped like animals or have a hut-like appearance called "tectiforms".

Art in all its forms

Art from South Asia is comparatively documented little less than their western counterparts. The cave sites of the Pachmarhi Hills in India amply showcase the life of the people during the Mesolithic period. Central and East Asia have numerous examples of art with carved figurines found in Malta. The archaeological site of Jiahu in China hosted bone flutes that represented the culture and their appreciation for music.

20,000 BCE: Human settlement

15,000 BCE: Cave paintings, Lascaux

Ice Age and Stone Age

Mammoths walked on Earth thousands of years ago.

The Ice Age occurred during the Pleistocene Epoch (2.6 million to 11,700 years ago) when huge glaciers formed and spread from the North Pole towards the south.

What are glaciers?

A glacier is a large mass of perennial (permanent) ice that is formed by the re-crystallisation of snow. During the Ice Age, such glaciers existed all over Canada, the USA and even the north-western part of Europe. Glaciers continue to exist even today, but are slowly melting as the temperature on earth has been increasing.

Sometimes, the ice was a thousand feet deep. But even in these sub-zero conditions, both plant and animal life existed. Some flowering plants and trees could be seen when the weather turned a little warm. Animals like reindeer and giant mammoths roamed the earth. Mammoths are similar in appearance to today's elephants.

What made Earth cold?

Scientists have not been able to state what exactly caused the Ice Age, but some believe that the change in Earth's orbital pattern could be one reason behind this. A few others believe that the reason could be attributed to the huge amounts of dust and fewer gases that could have made Earth cold.

Rise and fall of sea levels

The most recent Ice Age entered its coldest period about 22,000 years ago, when ice sheets covered a great part of North America and Northern Eurasia. As the seas froze, the sea level fell by over 100 m in certain places, exposing bridges of land between land masses. For example, the Bering Strait between Siberia and Alaska became a dry land, allowing animals such as mammoths and deer to move between Asia and North America. They were followed by human hunters, the first humans to colonise North America. When the climate became a little warm, the ice melted, sea levels rose and this as well as other land bridges disappeared. Conditions were extremely harsh for the people who lived near the ice sheets.

A melting glacier.

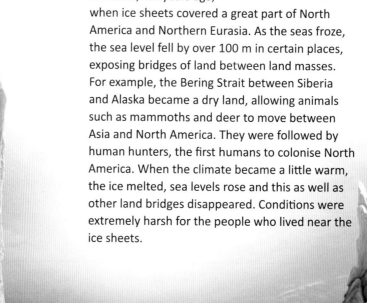

The Stone Age is divided into three separate periods: the Palaeolithic Period, the Mesolithic Period and the Neolithic Period. These divisions are based on the styles of different tools.

A Palaeolithic man using a spearhead against a wild animal for his defence.

The three age system

The term "Stone Age" was coined by the Danish scholar Christian J. Thomsen, who also came up with the "Three Age System". This system is based on the idea of three successive periods, namely the Stone Age, the Bronze Age and the Iron Age. Thomsen arrived at this system after observing the artefacts that were found in archaeological sites.

Stone Age tools.

The Stone Age began around 2.5 million years ago and continued till around 3300 BCE, when the Bronze Age began. The Stone Age is the earliest period of human development and the longest phase of humankind's history. It approximately coincides with the Pleistocene geologic period, beginning about two million years ago and ending in various places between 40,000 and 10,000 years ago, when it was succeeded by the Mesolithic period.

Stone Age tools

The first known tools were made by the Homo habilis around two million years ago. These were very simple tools made from pebbles. Over time, the tools became more advanced. People soon discovered that flint was one of the best tool-making materials available. It was extremely hard and it could be chipped into several pieces of various shapes and sizes. Stone Age people used flint blades to remove animal skin. The hides were used to make clothes, tents and bags. They would sew the pieces of skin together using needles made of antler or bone.

The tools during this period were made of stone, though other organic materials such as antler, bone, fibre, leather and even wood were used. These tools were used for the purpose of hunting as well as cutting roots, tubers and so on, to be used as food.

Stone Age man making a stone tool. As humans became smarter, they started to make even more complex tools.

1.8 million years ago: Ice Age

2.5 million years ago: Stone Age

FAST FACT

Did you know that when ice melted, different ridges, piles and other formations consisting of gravel, sand and soil were formed? The melting caused huge lakes to be formed and the sea level also rose, while some land sunk!

Palaeolithic Age

The Palaeolithic Age is also known as the "Old Stone Age", when the use of stone tools was very basic. This age saw the advent of the stone axe. During this period, the main task for humans was to protect themselves from wild animals and to gather food. Stones were also used to make fire.

Palaeoliths

The Lower Palaeolithic period occurred between 2,500,000 to 200,000 years ago. During this period, the hand axe was discovered. Stone flake tools also made an appearance. Around this time, humans preferred to live near water sources, enabling the formations of many river valleys and terraces. Palaeolithic people often lived together in small groups or societies called bands and survived on hunting and gathering plants. The artefacts found from this period are called "Palaeoliths".

Stone tools of the Palaeolithic Age

A sophisticated Lower Palaeolithic tradition, known as the chopper/chopping-tool industry, is widely distributed in the Eastern Hemisphere. This tradition is believed to have been the work of the hominine species named "Homo erectus". Although no fossil tools have yet been found, it is believed that Homo erectus perhaps made tools of wood and bone as well as stone. Some of the earliest known hand axes were found at Olduvai Gorge in Tanzania with the remains of Homo erectus. Besides the hand-axe tradition, a distinct and different stone-tool industry developed, which was based on flakes of stone. Special tools were made from worked flakes of flint that were carefully shaped.

2.5 million years ago: Palaeoliths

35,000 million years ago: Neanderthals

A man from the Palaeolithic Age.

An example of Palaeolithic stone tools.

FAST FACT

Did you know that the stone axe that was unearthed at the Lower Awash Valley in Ethiopia, Africa, was 3.4 million years old?

Life in different Palaeolithic periods

The people in the lower Palaeolithic period ate wild plants, fruits and meat. They were called "Neanderthals". During this age, people developed their creative skills, which was evident from the discovery of pendants, necklaces and other forms of jewellery made from shell, bone and ivory. During this period, humans showed an inclination towards arts. They engaged in religious and spiritual activities.

Hunting and gathering

Typically, women would gather wild plants and wood for fire, while men would hunt. Group hunting was also practiced for big animals like mammoths. Researchers believe that the people around this time knew about herbs and plants. Hunting was often geared to the seasonal killing of one or two species: mammoth or reindeer in Eurasia and wildebeest or zebra in Africa. Additionally, the Upper Palaeolithic bands of Europe and Northern Asia attained a degree of hunting efficiency unsurpassed even by advanced specialists such as the Eskimo or some of the North American Indians.

Technological advancement

This was a time of great advancement. The hunting populations became regionally specialised and improved their social and economic behaviour by using a greater variety of raw materials. They used the raw materials rigorously and introduced efficient means of obtaining food.

A group of Palaeolithic people living in a cave.

Growth of cultures

There was a growth of diverse human cultures: Aurignacians, Gravettian, Perigordian, Solutrean and Magdalenian. Aurignacians migrated from Asia to Europe. Solutreans came to Europe from the east. The Magdalean culture was perhaps the most impressive. Their remnants show that the Magdalenian people painted in caves and used tools made from microliths.

Different artifacts from the Palaeolithic Age.

Palaeolithic art

Two forms of Palaeolithic art are known to modern scholars: small sculptures and monumental paintings, incised designs and reliefs on the walls of caves. Evidence suggests that small sculptured pieces dominated the Upper Palaeolithic artistic traditions of Eastern Europe. The purpose of art in Palaeolithic life continues to be a debate.

FAST FACT

A group of humans called "Homo heidelbergensis" settled in Europe from Africa. They eventually evolved into Neanderthals.

A Venus figurine from the Palaeolithic Age.

Mesolithic Age

The Mesolithic Age is also known as the Middle Stone Age. It existed between the Palaeolithic period, where chipped stone tools were developed and the Neolithic Period, where polished stone tools were made.

Collection of different types of stone tools.

Tools of the Mesolithic Age

During this period, chipped stone tools called "microliths" were used. These microliths were very tiny stone tools, often of geometric shape, made from a bladelet and mounted singly or in series. The different tools included small flint microliths almost the same size as the human thumb. These microliths were used to make lightweight spears and arrows. The tools were made from bones and were to be used as fish hooks. Deer antlers were used for digging.

People of the Mesolithic Age

People during this period hunted, fished and lived along rivers and lakes. Pottery and the bow were developed during this period. Evidence of people living during this period was found in the Pyrenees region and later spread to Switzerland, Belgium and Scotland.

Tent houses

The nomadic Mesolithic people lived in temporary "tent houses" made from animal skins on poles. They were also known as hunter-gatherers because of the constant gathering and hunting for food. They hunted wild animals and gathered wild berries and nuts.

Evolving living conditions

Their nomadic style of living transformed due to favourable climate, good rainfall and warm atmosphere, which led to better food security conditions.

Climate during the Mesolithic Age

The retreat of the Pleistocene glaciers, the rising sea levels and the extinction of megafauna (large-bodied animals) was accompanied by a growth in forests and a major redistribution of animals and plants. After the climate stabilised, people moved northward into previously glaciated areas and adopted new subsistence methods. The climate during this period was warmer as compared to today and the landscape was made up of trees such as oak, elm and alders.

FAST FACT

The word "Epipaleolithic" is also used besides Mesolithic, which describes the various groups that lived during this period.

Mesolithic people are said to have forced most of the megafauna into extinction.

Pottery

The people of this time made distinctive pots with a point or knob base and flared rims. Evidence shows that the earliest forms of pottery from the Mesolithic era could be found in the areas around Lake Baikal in Siberia. There are diverse Mesolithic sites that include Star Carr, Newbury, Aveline's Hole and Howick House in England, Franchthi Cave in Greece, Cramond in Scotland, Mount Sandel in Ireland, Pulli Settlement in Estonia, Swifterbant culture in the Netherlands, Lepenski Vir in Serbia and Shigir Idol in Russia. The remnants of evidence found in these sites date back to 7500 BCE.

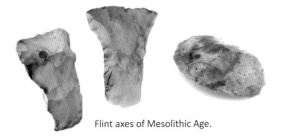

Flint axes of Mesolithic Age.

Cultures during the Mesolithic period

The Azilian culture is believed to be one of the early forms that emerged during the Late Paleolithic and Early Mesolithic Europe. It originated around the Pyrenees region and then spread to Europe. The culture that followed was the Tardenoisian culture, which also spread across Europe. The Maglemosian culture, named after a site in Denmark, is found in the Baltic region and North England. It was prevalent during the mid-Mesolithic period. It is here that hafted axes (an enhancement over the Palaeolithic hand axe) and bone tools were found. The Ertebolle culture during this period was centred on Denmark. The other cultures that closely followed the aforementioned cultures were the Campignian and Asturian cultures, which spread across the Middle East, while the Capsian culture spread across North Africa. The last one was the Natufian culture that brought about the beginning of the Neolithic era.

These pottery-making Mesolithic cultures can be found peripheral to the sedentary Neolithic cultures.

Emergence of farming

During this period, humans learnt the use of seeds of certain grasses, such as barley and wheat, as food. It is believed that humans may have thrown seeds into the soil and realised that these grow into plants. This is how humans began to grow their own crops. Humans also needed water for the crops to grow, so they began settling near plains with an extremely good supply of water.

End of the Mesolithic period

This period ended as farming spread across Europe. Cereal crops such as wheat and barley were introduced. Cattle and sheep were domesticated. Burial and ritualistic monuments began to be made and used for the first time. People also began making and using pottery full-fledged. It is unclear if this period ended with the influx of people who replaced the indigenous hunters and gatherers or with the initiation of new ideas and technologies, which was slowly adapted by the local population. Interestingly, this period was one of the most long-lived periods that lasted for over 6,000 years.

FAST FACT

It was during this period that "polished" stone was first discovered.

13

Neolithic Age

The word "Neo" comes from the Greek word "*Neos*", meaning "new". Therefore, the term Neolithic means "New Stone". The New Stone Age people used more sophisticated tools that were made from different types of stones such as jadeite or schist. Quite similar to the Old Stone Age, the New Stone Age humans also used stone tools.

Importance of wood

It was during this period that wood played a key role in the life of human beings. It was made a universally accepted building and hunting material. Canoes, paddles and other such materials were made during this period. Huts began to be made out of branches and stones. Slowly, the people settled in communities. Huts that seemed huddled together allowed for better defence. A contributing factor for this change was the emergence of agriculture.

Transition from food collecting to food cultivation

People slowly understood how to farm and domesticate animals. This created a huge shift in the way they lived because now they had a stable source of food and did not need to travel in search of food. This also gave them more time to explore other arts and crafts. The Neolithic people showed an interest in pottery, which mainly started in their quest to make vessels to store food. Soon, they also started living in bigger settlements and with larger communities.

Food cultivation

This period witnessed the cultivation of different crops like barley and wheat. The transition was long and gradual. It spread over Europe and the Indus Valley around 3000 BCE.

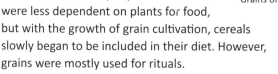

Grains of rye.

Around this time people were less dependent on plants for food, but with the growth of grain cultivation, cereals slowly began to be included in their diet. However, grains were mostly used for rituals.

Domestication of animals

Around this time, humans observed that some animals would come close to human habitation in search of food and would eat food that humans disposed. They learnt to tame these animals and use them for their own advantage. Animals like cow and sheep were domesticated during this period, to ensure a ready supply of meat, milk, wool and leather. The dog was the first animal that was domesticated during this period. Dogs would help humans and warn them of any danger as well.

3000 BCE: Food cultivation

3000 BCE: Stonehenge causeway enclosure

A seamless pattern with petroglyphs.

Neolithic people began to cook food.

Change in lifestyle

Farming and herding improved the living conditions of people to a great extent. Growing crops assured a continuous supply of food to man. Hunting provided him with a continuous supply of meat, milk and animal skin for clothing. Now that man did not have to be on the constant look out for food, he had time to improve and develop new skills. To take care of his crops, he needed to remain at one place for a long time. Therefore, permanent human settlements began to be established and community life began to emerge. Mud houses with thatched roofs began to be built during this time.

Neolithic houses had no windows, but had one doorway.

Emergence of communities

Communities began to emerge over time. The beginning of community life led to the concept of families being introduced. Families living in a Neolithic village were closely related and shared similar customs, beliefs and ways of worship. These people carried out farming, herding, hunting, gathering honey and fishing in groups. They jointly owned land, forests and water sources among other natural resources. As a result, there was equality of resource use and ownership.

Inventions and discoveries

People made significant progress during this time. Humans discovered basalt, a type of rock that they used to make tools which could be sharpened and polished. Humans also created many spindles and bone needles.

The problem of surplus food came about as humans started farming on a large scale. This is how they developed the idea of making pots. As time passed, Neolithic people learnt how to bake clay vessels on fire in which they could store liquids as well as cook.

Neolithic art

During this period, art was geometric and not representational, except among the hunter-fishers of the Taiga. Pots, which were always handmade, were painted in Southeastern Europe, Southern Italy and Sicily. In other places, they were adorned with carved, impressed or stamped patterns. Many designs are "skeuomorphic". This means that they enhance the pots' similarity to vessels of basketry or other material.

FAST FACT

Most clothing was made from skins of animals during this period. In fact, a well preserved corpse from 3300 BCE found in the Tyrolean Alps, revealed that Otzi the Iceman wore clothing made entirely from animal skins.

Stonehenge, England is believed to be a remnant of the Neolithic age.

Iron Age

Iron Age was a time when humans used tools and weapons made of iron. This age started somewhere in 1200 BCE in the middle and southeastern part of Europe. Around this time, iron was mixed with other materials to fortify it.

Iron anvil and tools.

Iron shaping

Iron was first extracted from rocks. This extracted material was worked into a shape by heating it repeatedly and then hammering it against an anvil. This process of shaping the raw material was called "smiting".

An anvil is a block of heavy iron that is flat on the top and has hollow inward facing sides on which different metals, particularly iron, can be hammered and made into different shapes.

Uses of iron

During the Iron Age, iron was not just used to form tools. It was used to make ploughs. These iron-tipped ploughs helped the farmers tackle heavy clay-like soil with ease, which led to significant progress in farming and the introduction of various new crops.

Iron was also used to make weapons and create armours like shields and helmets. These were created to protect the soldiers fighting in battles. The use of iron to create weapons also enabled people to create arms against each other for the first time, thus beginning the history of battles and warfare.

Iron was also used to make coins. In fact, coins were first minted in Britain around 100 BCE.

Discoveries and innovations

It was during the Iron Age that forts and bridges were being constructed for the first time. During this period, humans discovered the concept of mining to find salt and other precious minerals. The use of horse chariots was also first introduced during this period.

A new type of wheat was grown during this age. This wheat was called "bread wheat" and it was ground using rotary querns. Querns are stone tools that are used to grind (sometimes by hand) different kinds of materials like grains and cereals.

Shields were often decorated with a painted pattern or had an animal representation.

A quern stone with grain.

Life expectancy

During this period, the life expectancy of humans was just around 30 years, a hurdle that we have been able to overcome thanks to the advanced medical technology that we possess today. Back then, only around a quarter of the children born actually survived to experience adulthood.

During this period, people had small farms and increased farm yields. The Iron Age also marked the start of trading, when people began to sell and buy grains.

Weapons became a requirement for all households between 1900 and 1400 BCE, just when the tempering technique was invented. The Hittite rulers tried to keep the iron workings a secret, but after their downfall, migration movement ensured that the secret of iron forging soon spread to South Europe and the Middle East.

Emergence of farming

Before the Iron Age, human farming was dependent on temperate forests. Due to this, the cultivation of crops was limited. The Iron Age led to the creation of various tools that enhanced farming. Ploughs drawn by oxen also became common, thereby changing the agricultural patterns. These ploughs could dig through tough soil with ease, enabling the growth of new types of crops.

Villages were made more secure during the Iron Age. A farm during this period would have a hedge and ditch to deter any intruder, human or animal. Timber also became an equally important crop after wheat, barley and beans. It was used for fuel, building houses, carts, etc. As farming itself offered so many opportunities, everyone worked in the farms and very few chose to be artisans or take up another occupation.

During this period, animals herded were kept close to human dwellings.

However, it must be noted that the women during this period made skilled earthenware which were used for cooking as well as trading purposes. Women also did farmwork.

Their actual life expectancy, too, was short. In a family consisting of five girls and five boys, only two or three would actually survive and most people did not live longer than 45 years.

Iron tools used for farming.

An old iron pot and pewter spoon.

FAST FACT

Did you know that the Early Iron Age in Central Europe from 800 BCE to 500 BCE was called the "Hallstatt" period, while the later Iron Age was called La Tène?

Ancient Greek Civilisation

This civilisation existed from the end of the Mycenaean civilisation (1200 BCE) until Alexander the Great's death. The Greek empire spread from Greece to Europe. The Greeks were mainly involved in agriculture. Owing to a shortage of land, they were forced to look at sea-borne trade routes for more land. This led to clashes between the rich and poor, which paved the way for the beginning of democracy.

Olympic Games were held in elaborate stadiums.

Olympic Games

The first Olympic Games (as per records) were held in 776 BCE. As per a popular Greek legend, however, Heracles or the Roman Hercules, the son of Zeus, started the ancient Olympic Games. These Games were played every four years for around 1,200 years, but the Roman Emperor Theodosius I believed that the Games were unchristian and hence abolished them. Pierre de Coubertin proposed the Modern Olympic Games 1,500 years later.

Ancient Greeks started the Olympic Games. The first Olympic Games were held in 776 BCE at the Greek City of Olympia. It is said that Pheidippides ran from Athens to Sparta to request for help against the Persians before the Battle of Marathon.

Largest city-state

Athens, the largest city-state in Greece became a commercial centre and banker for the Greek world. During the fifth century BCE, the coin of Athens became the international currency of the Mediterranean.

People and their lives

Most Greeks lived in multi-storey apartment blocks equipped with bathrooms and toilets. Greek men wore a large piece of cloth that was draped over a woollen tunic, while women wore tunics that would reach their ankles. Both genders wore leather sandals on their feet.

Ancient Greece and the three periods

The three chronicled periods of Ancient Greece are the Archaic Period, from the 700 BCE to 480 BCE, when democracy emerged; the Classical Period, when philosophers like Socrates and Plato existed. This period ended with the death of Alexander the Great in 323 BCE and soon after this period came the Hellenistic Period from 323 to 146 BCE, when Greece was conquered by Rome.

The Parthenon was built for Athena, the patron Goddess of Athens.

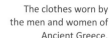

The clothes worn by the men and women of Ancient Greece.

FAST FACT

Did you know that the English word "politics" has its origin in the Greek word "polis", which stands for the term city state?

Democracy and its Origin in Greece

Theseus fighting the Centaur.

Athens was the one of the most known and biggest democracies. Citizens met, chose members of the government and formed a small council. The council discussed public matters by laying it before the assembly. In fact, this council also selected public officials whose positions were constantly rotated.

Greek mythology

Greek mythology would often feature very interesting characters, both human and beasts or creatures, to showcase different qualities from bravery to intelligence and greed to ego. Many of these creatures featured in stories of brave battles including the one with the "Minotaur" where the brave King Theseus kills the monster who devoured children and killed people with its deadly horns.

People during the ancient Greek civilisation

Women had very little independence during this period. They had slaves working for them who cooked, cleaned and looked after the crops. Slaves were a part and parcel of the ancient Greek life. Male slaves looked after the women, while the men were away. Ancient Greeks dressed in a long cotton cloth called "chiton". However, slaves were allowed to wear just a loincloth or a small cloth strip that was tied around the waist. The Greeks were polytheistic, that is, they believed in many Gods and Goddesses. The Greeks built statues of these Gods temples. One of these is the Parthenon temple, which was built for Goddess Athena, the protector of the city of Athens. Of these Zeus was the most important God.

Story of Medusa

Another battle story featured the horrible monster Medusa who had snakes for hair. She had tusks and a face that could turn anybody who saw it into stone! The brave warrior Perseus killed Medusa by wearing a helmet of invisibility. He looked at her reflection from his shiny shield. Greek mythology had many stories with interesting mythological characters such as the three-headed dog "Cerberus" who was the watchdog for the underworld. Another story was that of Pandora who was very curious about a box that Zeus had left behind. The box had a note that said "Do not open". But Pandora's curiosity made her open the box which is said to have released disease, pain and death in the world.

Perseus with the head of Medusa.

Aegean Civilisation

The Aegean Sea, a branch of the Mediterranean Sea, had the Greek mainland to its west and the island of Crete to its south. Present day Turkey was to its east. This region had entered the Bronze Age even as the rest of the region was in the Stone Age. Knossos in Crete Island was the home of King Minos the son of Zeus and Europa. Therefore, this civilisation is called the Minoan civilisation. There is evidence to prove that by 1600 BCE the Minoans had become predominant residents of the Aegean region.

Archaeological site of Phaistos, Crete, Greece.

Etymology

The origin of the name "Aegean" is said to come from the Greek town of Aegae or Aegea—named after the Queen of the Amazons who died at sea. Others believe that the name comes from "Aigaion"—which is the name of a sea goat. Some others believe that it is named after Aegeus, who is the father of Theseus who drowned in the sea believing his son had died during the Crete expedition on his way to defeat Minotaur.

Emergence of bronze

A lot of artefacts, especially pottery, from the Bronze Age has been found in Crete. Radiocarbon dating proves that these items were imported to Egypt as well. In fact, noted poet Homer's works contain certain customs of this civilisation, such as the warriors using bronze weapons and helmets.

Decoding the Aegean civilisation

The Aegean people lived near the sea. Much about them came to be known from the excavations carried out in sites near Crete. Unfortunately, many of the early writings found there could not be deciphered. It is known that an earthquake that devastated the Thera Island affected Cretan cities.

FAST FACT

Radiocarbon dating is a method of age determination of organic matter that is dependent on the decay of radiocarbon or carbon 14. Carbon 12 is formed continuously in nature by carbon's interaction with nitrogen 14 and neutrons. Tree rings are often used for radiocarbon measurements.

Bronze helmets with tusks from the wild boar.

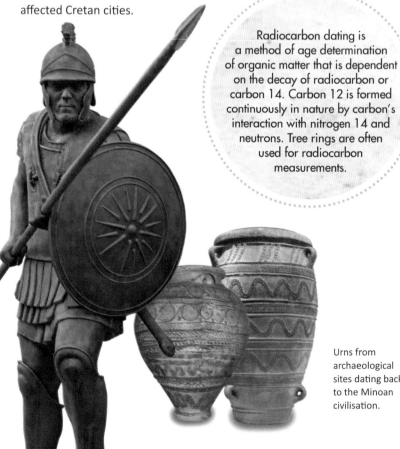

Urns from archaeological sites dating back to the Minoan civilisation.

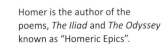

Homer is the author of the poems, *The Iliad* and *The Odyssey* known as "Homeric Epics".

Greek literature

The Greeks have a rich history of literature. Greek literature includes the form of epic poems like Homer's *"The Iliad"* and *The Odyssey*. A theory suggests that Homer did not make the stories in these poems, rather just wrote them down. The content is said to be from legends that other poets and bards had been narrating for hundreds of years. Other works such as Hesiod's *"Theogony"* or poems by Archilochus and Sappho were also from this culture. Next, come the plays that were essentially either tragedies or comedies. Among these were the ones written by Aeschylus or Sophocles and Euripides. Menander and Aristophanes wrote comedies. Philosophy also originated in Greece from the philosophical writings of Plato. Aristotle, a student of Plato, also wrote philosophical prose.

Ancient Greek sarcophagus decorated with scenes from *The Iliad*.

Commodity production

The Aegean archipelago produced various commodities including grapes, figs, raisins, honey, wheat, vegetables, wine and certain herbs. Marble became an intrinsic aspect of their commerce. With the export of marble, the ancient Greeks became quite wealthy.

Prominent civilisations

Two different civilisations were prominent during this period, the Minoan and Mycenaean. A devastating earthquake resulted in the complete destruction of cities in Crete. By 1400 BCE, the Minoan civilisation completely disappeared. The Mycenaean's invaded the Greek mainland. They built huge fortresses, which provided refuge during battles and wars. The Dorians defeated them. The Dorians had a distinct dialect and were subdivided into tribes called "Dymanes", "Pamphyloi" and

Round tower of Spinalonga fortress, Crete, Greece.

"Hylleis". They brought about the infamous "dark age", which spread poverty. This lasted for nearly 300 years. In 750 BCE, the Ionians were responsible for introducing cultural elements including writing, art and reading. A new period now known as the Hellenic period emerged, which made the Greek civilisations, one of the most powerful.

1600 BCE: Aegean Civilisation

1400 BCE: Minoan Civilisation ends

Hellenistic Age

Back in 336 BCE, Alexander the Great began his rule over the Greek kingdom of Macedonia. He died 13 years later. He had built an impressive empire that stretched from Greece all the way to India. This great expansion spread Greek ideas and culture to different parts of the world. This period was called the Hellenistic Age. The word Hellenistic originates from "Hellazein", which means "to speak Greek" or "to identify with the Greeks". The period lasted until the Roman troops began to conquer all the territories that the Macedonian king had ruled over.

Alexander the Great.

It was during King Philip's reign that the expansion of the Macedonian empire started. Advanced tools of warfare aided them in this pursuit. These include the long-range catapults that had pikes called "sarissas" and were almost 16 feet long that were used as spears by the soldiers. King Philip was assassinated and his son Alexander took over the imperial expansion project. After Alexander's death, the conquered lands were divided into three powerful dynasties including the Ptolemies of Egypt, Antigonids of Greece and Macedonia and the Seleucids of Syria and Persia.

A silhouette of Macedonian soldiers.

Warfare during this age

Towards the end of the Classical period in 360 BCE, the city-states were very fragile and jumbled owing to 200 years of fighting when the Athenians fought against the Persians. Then, the Spartans fought against the Athenians and finally the Thebans and Persians fought against the Athenians. This constant warfare made it easy for Macedonia to rise to power under the leadership of King Philip II.

Ancient Greek warrior in combat.

Spread of culture

Alexander was responsible for the spread of the Greek culture throughout the Persian Empire. However, Alexander gave importance to the local culture and ensured that the local customs continued. He was one of those kings who embraced local customs and encouraged his soldiers to marry Persian women. Alexander is said to be responsible for the Hellenistic age.

FAST FACT

Did you know that in the Hellenistic age items like ivory, gold, ebony, spices, cotton and sugars were imported from India?

A sculpture from the Hellenistic period.

The Hellenistic People

During this age there was a constant need to show and display the wealth for everyone to see—as a result, elaborate palaces were built. Museums, zoos, universities and libraries were sponsored. The university at Alexandria was home to noted mathematicians such as Archimedes, Euclid and Apollonius. People spoke a language called "Koine"—a colloquial form of Greek. Some people joined religions like the cults of Fortune and Isis that promised its followers wealth and immortality. This period ended in 31 BCE when in the Battle of Actium, Romans defeated Marc Antony's fleet.

End of the Hellenistic period

The Hellenistic Period ended in 31 BCE. With the death of Alexander the Great, there was no strong leader left to protect his kingdoms. This was brought about by the conquest of the remaining Hellenistic kingdoms by the Roman Empire. The wars between its rulers also weakened the Hellenistic kingdoms, leaving them open for the attacks by the Romans.

Growth of cultures

This was a time of great learning in different fields from math and arts to architecture. It was a time when Archimedes, Hero and Euclid made discoveries. This period was also a time of relative peace, which is one of the reasons why travel and trade grew. Antipater from the city of Sidon is credited with a poem that sites down the Seven Wonders of the World. He picked these buildings and statues for the beautiful architecture and art that they exhibited. The different places of prominence in the Hellenistic period include Alexandria in Egypt, Antioch in Syria and Pergamum in Asia Minor. An interesting fact is that though none of these cities were in Greece, they were all influenced by Greek architecture.

Greek architecture was also visible in the universities of Taxila and Nalanda in India.

336 BCE: Alexander's rule over Macedonia

31 BCE: The Hellenistic Period ends

FAST FACT

The Hellenistic Period is usually defined as a transition period between Alexander the Great's death and the expansion of the Roman Empire.

The fortress in Alexandria, Egypt.

Ancient Italic Period

Ancient Italic people inhabited Italy prior to the Roman Italy, as we know it today. It was a region that was greatly influenced by Greek culture. In fact, Etruscans were a powerful nation and it was them who taught the Romans the alphabet and numbers.

Etruscan gravestones, "Pietra fetida" funerary sphinx, middle sixth century BCE.

Carvings of ancient Etruscans.

The Etruscans

The Greeks knew the Etruscans as Tyrsenoi, while the Latins called them Etrusci. The Etruscan region consisted of the areas that bordered the Tyrrhenian Sea in the west, the Tiber River in the south and east, while in the north was the Arno River. This region was rich in metal ores such as copper, iron and tin.

They dominated the western coasts of Italy and prospered. The Greek connect started around 775 BCE when the Greek Islanders of Euboea moved near the Bay of Naples and settled there. The Etruscans traded with the Greeks. They traded lumber and fur to the east and purchased spices and perfume. The Etruscans had a government system, where the control was held by the central government.

The origin of the Etruscan civilisation is unknown. However, the people from this period are said to have come from the Villanovan culture or from invasions that took place in the East of this area. Etruscan expansion was focussed both to the north beyond the Apennines and into Campania.

The Toga

The Etruscans created the Toga, which became the official costume of the Romans. It was made from a semi circular white wool cloth piece. Only emperors or senators used purple coloured clothing. They were known for their gold and semi-precious stoned jewellery. These ancient Italic people played board games including checkers and chess. They influenced Roman architecture, particularly the grid plan city system. The Etruscans followed a Polytheistic religion. The Etruscan language does not figure in any literary work. There is a playwright named Volnius who wrote the "Tuscan Tragedies".

FAST FACT

Did you know that the Ancient Romans used oil instead of soap while bathing? A metal tool called "strigil" was used to scrape off the oil that was scrubbed into the skin.

Ancient roman man and woman wearing the Toga.

A commemorative plaque.

Etruscan inscriptions

These inscriptions were found in the Zagreb mummy wrapping during the nineteenth century in Egypt. The wrapping was a book of linen cloth and was cut into strips and wrapped around the mummy. It had some 1300 words written in black ink and is known as the longest existing Etruscan text. More than 10,000 Etruscan inscriptions were found on vases, statues and jewellery as well as on tombstones. But there is still no clarity on the pronunciation of the Etruscan letters. There was also some evidence that they had some music notation system as well. The Etruscan language was in use by the people up until the first century CE, but later became the language in which priests and scholars conversed and studied.

Ancient Italic people and their customs

Religion became a uniting factor for the diverse Etruscan cities. These people had a strong belief in life after death. The beliefs can be amply gauged from the frescoed paintings in Tarquinia in northern Rome. The Etruscans were deeply influenced by mysticism, which we could even call "superstition".

Unlike Greek and Roman societies, women sat with their husbands to eat at banquets and had their own possessions. They were also very active in politics. The Etruscans were both economically and geographically rich. They controlled the Tyrrhenian Sea, and thereby controlled the Mediterranean and the continent of Europe.

Downfall of the Etruscan cities

After 400 years of Etruscan rule, they could not hold against the force of the reorganised Romans, who had managed to unite themselves and gained over their opponents quite easily. By 265 BCE the Romans had already claimed the Etruscan cities.

FAST FACT

Did you know that the Tuscan region is named after the Etruscans? Tuscany comes from the Latin word "Tuscanus", which is derived from the word "Tuscas", meaning an Etruscan.

Ancient Etruscan art.

Etruscan warrior riding a chariot.

Etruscan Roman archeology museum.

Barbarian Invasions

There are numerous reasons that led to the barbaric invasion. One of them was the decline of the Roman military and also lead poisoning through water and food. Few historians claimed this could have caused lower births, anaemia and gout among the Roman citizens. Another cause was the split of the empire and the failing economy. Even as the Roman Empire got divided, not a single emperor could withstand the invasion from the different tribes of Northeastern Europe.

Anglo Saxon stone monument

Germanic tribe invasion

In 410, Rome was attacked by Germanic tribes who moved across the Roman Empire in a destructive and barbaric manner which earned them the name. These tribes settled down over the vast empire in different regions. For instance, the Angles and Saxons settled in England, while the Franks in France and Lombards made Italy their hometown. The Huns were a nomadic group who plundered the Roman Empire, but eventually lived in Eastern Europe, Central Asia and the Caucasus.

The Franks, Angles and Saxons

The Franks ruled in the northern part of France from 481 to 511. Clovis ruled over the tribe and also followed Christianity. In time, the Franks married the native Gallo-Roman people and soon the cultures merged. While in Spain, the Alans, Sueves and Vandals occupied Spain after crossing the Pyrenees, but when the Visigoth King crushed Sueves tribes, Spain came under the Visigoth rule. In England, the Saxons conquered

Sussex in 492 and by the sixth century Angles and Saxons conquered an entire part in Eastern England. Not all Saxons and Angles were interested in war as some even traded with the Romans. Pope Gregory managed to convert the Angles and Saxons to Christianity.

FAST FACT

These people were originally from a place called "Gaul", which was the name given to their military area. They were believed to have come from a common background and had similar religious faith.

An artist's imagination of the Franks, Angles and Saxons.

Attila the Hun

Being a warrior race, the Huns were very good horse riders. They were feared because they plundered kingdoms and were very violent. Led by King Attila, they were dreaded by the European Empire. The Huns devastated the Gaul region and the other barbarians joined the Goths and Franks. The Burgundians joined hands to defeat the Huns at the "Battle of the nations"—as the battle was called.

Defeat of the Huns

They were defeated, but Attila did not give up, he marched through Italy, leaving in his wake a devastated Rome. Pope Leo I, assisted by St Peter and St Paul were left with the job of making Attila see sense, and thereby ensured that he halted and did not go further with his plundering of Rome. It also did not help that the Huns soon found themselves troubled by famine and plague and the numbers in their armies began to drop. Attila's retreat was soon followed by his death—he died after he choked to death from a nosebleed. After the death of Attila, his sons split the empire amongst them, but the Huns never returned to their former glory. Soon, this clan mixed with others including Germans and Slavs.

Decline of Rome

In 537 CE, the aqueducts (water supply stations) of Rome were destroyed and the Romans died without water. The population fell by almost 90 per cent, putting the city to an end. Gibbon, the historian wrote in his *History of the Decline and Fall of the Roman Empire*, "the decline of Rome was

Painting of the Huns attack in Turkey.

the natural and inevitable effect of immoderate greatness. The story of its ruin is simple and obvious, instead of inquiring why the Roman Empire was destroyed we should rather be surprised that it existed for so long."

Romulus and Remus

According to an old legend, Rome was founded by twin brothers named Romulus and Remus in 735 BCE. At birth, they were left to die at the bank of the Tiber river in Italy. They were saved by a she-wolf who also fed them. They were later discovered by a shepherd who raised them. Years later, as adults, they decided to build a city in honour of the she-wolf that rescued them. The city was to be built on the Palatine Hill where they were found by the she-wolf.

410 CE: Germanic Tribe invasion on Rome

537 CE: Decline of the Roman Empire

A mosaic depicting the Sword of God, the legendary weapon of Attila the Hun.

Old map of Barbarian kingdoms before Clovis I.

FAST FACT

Rome was named after Romulus, the first king of Rome. He won this title after a quarrel with his brother Remus, where the latter was killed.

Configuration of the Roman Empire

She-wolf suckling Romulus and Remus - the traditional founders of the city and empire of Rome.

The Roman Empire was a feudalistic monarchy and it consisted of parts of France, Italy, Slovenia, Austria, Belgium, Germany, Holland, Luxembourg and the Czech and Slovak Republics. In 753 BCE, Rome's first king Romulus was credited with being the founder of Rome. Over the next hundred years, the Roman Empire grew into a successful and powerful city. Till up to 117 CE, the Roman Empire had spread to include Italy, the Mediterranean, Europe, England, Wales and even parts of Scotland.

Origins of Rome

Another legend on the origin of Rome says that the brothers could not agree with where the new city should be built. They had each picked a place. They decided to consult with some birds to find out who had picked the better place. Romulus won, and thus became the king of Rome. Rome began developing during the sixth century BCE near the River Tiber. Close to the river were the seven hills of Rome: Capitol, Palatine, Caelian, Esquiline, Viminal, Quirinal and Aventine. Soon, the hills were cleared of trees to make room for houses and temples on its hilly slopes. Communities started living in these areas and trade also began.

Roman Empire and the Romans

The Romans were decent architects and engineers. They built many elements like roads and walls. They also built aqueducts that could transport water for public baths and toilets. The farming methods were very advanced and had used water mills, manure and mechanical reapers. They built fantastic roads; in fact the saying that "All roads lead to Rome" comes from the road that was built in London to Wroxeter in Shropshire.

FAST FACT

Did you know that even as the Romans built their huge empire, they owed its speed to its army that had the ability to march up to 40 km a day?

A picture from an archaeological site of Ancient Rome.

Remains of the public baths in Pompeii.

Antique illustration of Roman Forum, Italy.

753 BCE: First Roman king, Romulus

1453 BCE: End of the Roman Empire

Public baths

They had big public baths and toilets where 60 people could be easily accommodated. The Romans invented concrete and they were the ones who used it to make the Pantheon that still exists even today. They liked to live a luxurious life, which explains the villas that had bath suites, mosaic floors and under floor heating.

Religion followed by the people

They believed in the power that God held over nature; hence, they would perform different sacrifices. It was only during the rule of Emperor Constantine that Christianity became the religion of the empire. Before the spread of Christianity, Romans believed in many gods and goddesses like the Greeks. All of these gods were said to have come from one family and represented different things.

End of the Roman Empire

Everything from anarchy to barbaric invasions to plague, the decline of the empire slowly began during the third century, but eventually it ended after a few centuries. While the Eastern Roman Empire was called Constantinople and lasted till 1453, the Western Empire was devastated by the barbaric invasions.

The once strong Roman military slowly became inefficient and failed to safeguard the borders of the vast city. The internal rebellions failed the government which was unable to collect taxes and safeguard the economy. Foreign powers such as the Visigoths also weakened the Roman Empire.

FAST FACT

The Senate in the USA is in charge of making laws there. It is actually named after the Roman Senate.

The gladiator

The Romans enjoyed gladiator contests complete with swordsmen. The gladiators would generally be prisoners or slaves. Each gladiator had his individual way of fighting and each style would be different. Armed with swords and armours, the gladiators would fight till either one of the men died. Those who were about to lose would beg for pardon from death, but it was up to the emperor and the crowd to decide if the gladiator would live or die. This made the contests very thrilling and exciting for the crowd.

The contests were held in big amphitheatres and people would come to watch the fights between them. Sometimes the men would also fight with animals. Men in armour would fight against animals like bears, bulls, alligators, lions and tigers.

A Roman gladiator.

29

Civilisations of Africa

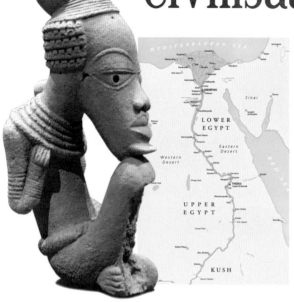

Besides the Egyptian civilisation there was another great civilisation that grew during pre-historic times. It emerged in Nubia, currently Northern Sudan, which existed around 2000 BCE. It was called the "Kingdom of Kush". It was conquered by Egypt in 1500 BCE.

Diverse Africa

Africa can be divided culturally between sub-Saharan Africa and the northern countries from Egypt to Morocco. The northern countries mostly follow the Arabic culture. The southern parts of the Sahara belong to the Bantu group. Within Africa there are divisions between French Africa and the rest of Africa, there are groups who still follow the traditional living style of Africans till date.

A new capital

During the third century BCE, the capital of Kush moved to Meroe, which was on the banks of the river Nile. This city became an important centre for iron working. The people of this region were known as the "Nok". Their culture developed until 200 CE. These people engaged in occupations such as iron mining and smelting of clay. They used the iron to make tools such as hoes and axes. They used the tools to clear land for cultivation. They also made iron arrowheads, spears and knives.

The Nok people from the Meroe region.

Kush nobility

The nobles lived along the River Nile. They believed that they were similar to Egyptians, although the Egyptians would not accept this. They lived in houses similar to the Egyptians and worshipped the same Gods, with few Gods of their own such as the three-headed lion God. They had queens as rulers rather than kings or pharaohs. They mummified their dead. They built tombs with flat roofs.

The commoners

The common people also mummified their dead copying the nobility. They also worshipped the same Gods. However, they did not consider themselves as Egyptians. The common people lived in villages. They were farmers and were proud of their village. Each village had a leader, but the leader was not a king, queen or chief. The leader did not rule; rather, the leader suggested and led discussions. The villagers took decisions together along with their leader.

FAST FACT

The "Nok" is a name given to the people from Meroe. It came from the art of this region, which later influenced West African art.

Karima Pyramids, Sudan.

Indicators of Early Civilisations

Cave paintings are paintings that are found on the walls and ceilings of caves. These prehistoric paintings were made over 40,000 years ago. They are an important source of information about the early civilisations. Many such cave paintings have been found in Europe and Asia. While very little is known about why the paintings were made, historians believe that the cave paintings were a way of expression for the prehistoric people, either to communicate with each other or as part of a religious custom.

Cave paintings in the Cueva de las Manos, Patagonia, Argentina.

FUN FACT

The oldest known cave paintings were discovered on the island of Sulawesi in Indonesia. The paintings are around 35,000 years old.

Universal similarity

The paintings are remarkably similar around the world, with animals being common subjects of the cave paintings. The paintings often include images of human hands, mostly hand stencils. Scientists believe that to make the stencils, the early humans held a hand to the wall and blew pigment on it.

The paintings on the wall of the shelters date to the Mesolithic period. They consist of geometric patterns and figures made in red and white, with some use of yellow and green. They depict the daily lives of the people with scenes of childbirth, dancing, drinking and rituals of burial among others.

Paintings at Bhimbetka

The Bhimbetka rock shelters in India are an archaeological site dating back to the Stone Age. Located at the foothills of the Vindhya Mountains in the south of the central Indian plateau, the Bhimbetka rock shelters are five clusters of natural rock shelters. Historians estimate that human beings occupied the shelters more than 100,000 years ago.

Prehistoric rock petroglyphs in Usgalimol, India.

Lion plate with lion man and other bushman prehistoric rock engravings.

Indus and Sarasvati Civilisations

Mohenjo Daro is a city in the Indus valley civilisation that was built around 2600 BCE and flourished till 1900 BCE. It was discovered in the 1920s.

The Indus valley civilisation was one of the largest civilisations of the ancient world, bigger than Sumer and even Egypt. The Indus valley civilisation was discovered during the 1920s. Its two great cities were Harappa and Mohenjo Daro. Each of these cities had a population of more than 40,000. It had a well organised system of trade. Merchants traded grains along with other agricultural produce that grew along the fertile river banks.

River Sarasvati

The Indus valley civilisation was one of the world's major ancient civilisations that included Egypt, Mesopotamia, South Asia and China. All these civilisations emerged on the banks of rivers. For example, Mesopotamia flourished on the banks of the river Tigris and Euphrates.

The Indus valley civilisation developed on the banks of the river Indus—Sarasvati. There is evidence to prove that similar to the Mesopotamians, the people from the Indus valley civilisation were also culturally rich and seemed to have had some form of writing in existence.

Course of Sarasvati

The Sarasvati River is the Ghaggar stream that ends in the Thar Desert. It used to flow into the Arabian Sea till 1900 BCE when it dried up because the Yamuna changed course and started flowing into the river Ganga.

Old map of the Indian sub-continent, 1867 showing rivers.

Decline of the civilisation

Unfortunately, from 2000 BCE, the Indus valley civilisation began to decline. This is attributed to the devastating floods that destroyed the crops or because the river Indus changed its course making the once fertile land barren. Interestingly, it is believed that overgrazing may have also contributed to the decline as the land became too dry, rendering it impossible to grow any crops.

Confluence of Zanskar and Indus rivers – Leh, Ladakh.